W9-BVQ-005

LOOKING AT MAPS AND GLOBES

by Rebecca Olien

Content Consultant

Laura McCormick
Cartographer
XNR Productions Inc.

Children's Press®
An Imprint of Scholastic Inc.
New York   Toronto   London   Auckland   Sydney
Mexico City   New Delhi   Hong Kong
Danbury, Connecticut

Library of Congress Cataloging-in-Publication Data
Olien, Rebecca.
  Looking at maps and globes/by Rebecca Olien.
      p. cm.—(Rookie read-about geography)
  Includes bibliographical references and index.
  ISBN 978-0-531-28964-8 (lib. bdg.) — ISBN 978-0-531-29288-4 (pbk.)
  1. Maps—Juvenile literature. 2. Globes—Juvenile literature. I. Title.
  GA105.6.O4 2013
  912.01'4—dc23   2012003192

SCHOLASTIC, CHILDREN'S PRESS, ROOKIE READ-ABOUT®, and associated logos
are trademarks and/or registered trademarks of Scholastic Inc.

1 2 3 4 5 6 7 8 9 10 R 22 21 20 19 18 17 16 15 14 13

Photographs © 2013: age fotostock/View Stock: 24; Alamy Images: 8 (Aerial Archives),
cover (Ed Bock/Corbis Bridge), 10 (TongRo Images Inc.); iStockphoto: 22, 29 top right
(Don Bayley), 28 (Neil_J); Media Bakery/Ronnie Kaufman: 16; National Geographic
Stock/Jason Edwards: 6; PhotoEdit/Myrleen Pearson: 12, 29 bottom right; Rita Lascaro:
18, 29 top left; Scholastic, Inc.: 20, 29 bottom left; Shutterstock, Inc.: 30, 31 (mart),
4 (photobank.kiev.ua), 26 (strelka), 14 (Volina).

Table of Contents

Finding the Way

People look at maps to find places. Maps show the way to go.

These kids want to see the lions. How do they know where to go? They look at a map of the zoo.

8

How Maps Work

Look at a map. It is like looking down from the sky. Here is what a city looks like from a plane.

Here is a map of the same city. Can you find the roads and water?

Many Kinds of Maps

There are many kinds of maps. A world map can show all the countries in the world.

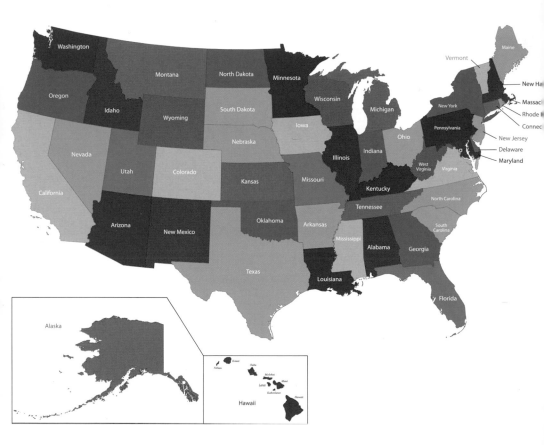

Washington
Montana
North Dakota
Minnesota
Oregon
Idaho
Wyoming
South Dakota
Wisconsin
Michigan
Vermont
Maine
New Ham
New York
Massac
Rhode I
Connec
New Jersey
Delaware
Maryland
Nevada
Utah
Colorado
Nebraska
Iowa
Illinois
Indiana
Ohio
Pennsylvania
West Virginia
Virginia
California
Kansas
Missouri
Kentucky
North Carolina
Arizona
New Mexico
Oklahoma
Arkansas
Tennessee
South Carolina
Mississippi
Alabama
Georgia
Texas
Louisiana
Florida

Alaska

Niihau
Kauai
Oahu
Molokai
Maui
Lanai
Kahoolawe
Hawaii
Hawaii

14

A map can show one country. This is a map of the United States. Can you find the state where you live?

People use road maps when driving to a place. The map shows what roads to take.

Kitchen

Front room

Living room

Bedroom

Floor plans are maps of indoor places. This floor plan is of a home. How is it like your home?

Map Key

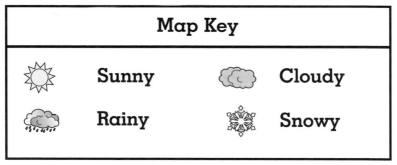

☀	**Sunny**	☁	**Cloudy**
🌧	**Rainy**	❄	**Snowy**

A weather map shows where it might rain or snow. Look at this weather map. What kind of weather do you see?

Globes

People look at globes to see
the world. A globe is round
like Earth.

You can see all around the world with a globe. Spin a globe to see how Earth turns.

A globe shows the world's water and land. Do you see oceans on the globe?

Looking at maps and globes helps people learn about places. What will you use to find your way today?

Words You Know

floor plans

globes

weather map

world map

29

Look at this world map. Where is the water? Where is the land? Can you find the country where you live? What other countries are near it?

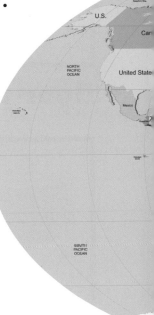

Visit this Scholastic Web site for
more information on maps and globes:
www.factsfornow.scholastic.com
Enter the keywords **Maps and Globes**

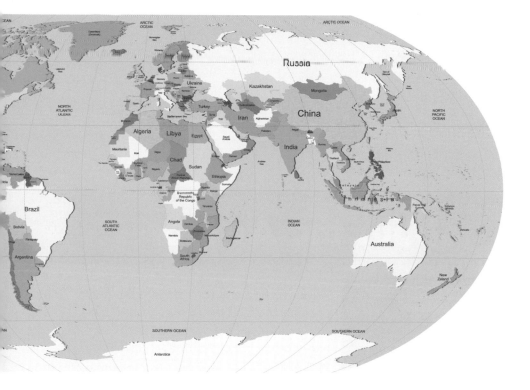

Index

About the Author

Rebecca Olien is a teacher and author of more than 50 books for educators and children. You can often find her studying maps or twirling a globe to find new places to go.